Ancient Myths
The Wooden Horse of Troy

Written by
John Malam

Created and designed by
David Salariya

Illustrated by
Peter Rutherford

Sandy Creek
NEW YORK

An Imprint of Sterling Publishing
387 Park Avenue South
New York, NY 10016

Series creator: David Salariya
Author: John Malam
Editors: Michael Ford, Nadia Higgins
Illustrations: Peter Rutherford

ISBN 978-1-4351-5117-8

Manufactured in Heyuan, Guangdong Province, China
Lot #:
2 4 6 8 10 9 7 5 3 1
06/13

Table of Contents

The World of Ancient Mythology 4

Introduction 5

Troy: Built with the Gods' Help 6

The Judgment of Paris 8

Paris Takes Helen to Troy 10

The Fleet Sails to Troy 12

The Siege of Troy 14

Let the Battle Begin! 16

Achilles Kills Hector 18

The Death of Achilles 20

The Wooden Horse of Troy 22

The Fall of Troy 24

The Return of the Heroes 26

The End of the Story? 28

Glossary 30

Who's Who 31

Index 32

The World of Ancient Mythology

The ancient Greek civilization was one of the greatest the world has witnessed. It spanned nearly 2,000 years, until it was eventually overwhelmed by the Roman Empire in the second century B.C. At its height, the ancient Greek world extended far beyond what we know as modern Greece.

We owe much to the ancient Greeks. They were great scientists, mathematicians, dramatists, and philosophers. They were also brilliant storytellers. Many of the tales they told were in the form of poetry, often thousands of lines long. The Greeks wrote poems on almost all kinds of human experiences—love, friendship, war, revenge, history, and even everyday life. The most famous of the poems that have passed down to us are the epic tales of courage and warfare, where brave heroes struggle and suffer against great odds.

A map showing the ancient Greek mainland, surrounding islands, and territories

What is incredible is that until the eighth century B.C., the Greeks had no recognized form of writing. All of their stories, lengthy as they were, were handed down from generation to generation by word of mouth. The people who passed on these tales were often professional storytellers, who would perform in town squares or public theaters. Often several versions of the same myth existed, depending on who told it and when. What follows is one version of the Wooden Horse of Troy.

If you need help with any of the names, go to the pronunciation guide on page 31.

Introduction

Gather round and hear my story. I am the rhapsode—the teller of stories. You may all have heard of the great siege at Troy—the beautiful woman who caused the conflict, the brave warriors who fought and fell, and the trickery that ended it all.

I come this day from far away
With a tale to tell that spins a spell,
Which you will hear—if you draw near—
Of times of old and heroes bold.

So gather round and hear my story,
Which I will weave from ancient glory
By joining threads from start to end
That you may pass on to a friend.

Troy: Built with the Gods' Help

My story begins long, long ago, in an age when immortal gods mixed with humans on Earth. The great god Zeus sent his son Apollo and his brother Poseidon to work among men. For the two gods, this was a punishment for rebelling against Zeus. For one whole year, Apollo and Poseidon worked for Laomedon, the king of Troy. With the help of Aeacus, one of the humans, they built strong walls around the city.

Laomedon had promised his famous immortal horses as payment for the gods' help, but he broke his promise when the work was done. Apollo sent a plague upon Troy, and Poseidon ordered a sea serpent to attack the city. Laomedon appealed for help, and an oracle told him he must sacrifice his daughter, Hesione, to the serpent. He could not bear to lose her, though. Instead, he promised his horses to whoever killed the monster. This brave deed fell to the hero Hercules. Hercules killed the monster, but Laomedon broke his promise again.

The snakes that foretold the future

When the walls of Troy were built, three snakes slithered to the top of them. The two snakes that climbed the parts built by the gods fell down dead. However, the snake that climbed the wall built by Aeacus slid into the city. Apollo said it was a sign that Troy would be taken over by the descendants of Aeacus.

Ask the storyteller

What did Hercules do?

Hercules was angry because Laomedon had not given up his horses. He left Troy, but returned many years later to kill Laomedon and his sons. Hesione successfully pleaded with Hercules to spare her brother, Podarces, who from then on was known as Priam, the new king of Troy.

Build high! Build strong!

The Judgment of Paris

As time went by, King Priam and his wife, Hecabe, had a son called Paris. However, before the child's birth, Hecabe had a nightmare that she would give birth to a flaming torch. She thought this was a bad omen and was afraid of her new son, so she left baby Paris to die on a mountain. But he didn't. Luckily, he was found by a shepherd who raised him as his own son.

Paris grew into a fine young man who worked as a shepherd. One day, as he tended his flock, he came upon three goddesses—Hera, Athena, and Aphrodite. They were arguing over a golden apple, upon which was written, "For the most beautiful." They asked Zeus to decide, but he ordered Paris to be the judge. Hera offered to give him all of Asia and Europe if he chose her. Athena vowed to make him a great warrior, and Aphrodite promised him Helen, the most beautiful woman in the world. Overcome with love for Helen, Paris gave the apple to Aphrodite.

The Apple of Strife

A goddess called Eris had thrown the apple amongst the goddesses. She was angry because they had been invited to a wedding and she had not. Eris knew they would argue over who was the most beautiful of them all.

Ask the storyteller

Did Paris choose wisely?

Poor Paris. He allowed himself to be tempted by the bribes of the goddesses and let his heart rule his head. His love for Helen was strong, but in choosing her, his fate was doomed, as was that of the city of Troy.

I choose your gift, goddess Aphrodite.

Paris Takes Helen to Troy

Ten years had passed since Paris's meeting with the three goddesses. During this time, Paris had returned to Troy and was accepted back into his real family.

Meanwhile, many men had asked for Helen's hand in marriage. However, her father, the Spartan king Tyndareus, wanted to make sure Helen would be well cared for. He made all his daughter's suitors swear they would always protect her. After this, Helen chose a noble called Menelaus as her husband.

Through all this, Aphrodite had not forgotten her promise to Paris. She waited until Menelaus was away from Sparta, then took Paris to meet Helen. With a little help from Aphrodite, Paris led Helen to his ship at night, loaded it with stolen treasure, then sailed away back to Troy.

When Menelaus discovered what had happened, he was furious.

A last resort

At first, Menelaus tried to get Helen back by peaceful means. He went to Troy and pleaded for her return, but his demands were rudely rejected. From then on, he knew that the only way to win Helen's freedom was by defeating the Trojans in war.

Ask the storyteller

Why did Helen go with Paris?

Aphrodite cast a powerful spell over Helen, making her fall in love with Paris. Some say the goddess made Paris look like Menelaus, tricking Helen into believing she was with her husband.

The Fleet Sails to Troy

Menelaus visited his brother, Agamemnon, king of Mycenae, to ask for help. Agamemnon called on all the men who had sworn to protect Helen. In this way, the Greeks assembled an army with Agamemnon as their leader.

Agamemnon gathered 1,000 ships at the port of Aulis, ready to take the Greek army across the sea to Troy. However, a prophet named Calchas said the fleet must not sail until Achilles had joined them, because Troy could only be conquered with the hero's help. Calchas, who was skilled in reading signs sent by the gods, saw a snake eat nine sparrows and then turn to stone. He said this omen meant Troy would only be captured after 10 years of war. Calchas's next prophecy was grim: Agamemnon must sacrifice his own daughter, Iphigeneia, to please the gods. So, Agamemnon called the girl to him, pretending she was to be married to Achilles, but this was just a trick. She was soon sacrificed on an altar. After this, the wind blew strong and the fleet set sail to Troy.

Philoctetes is abandoned

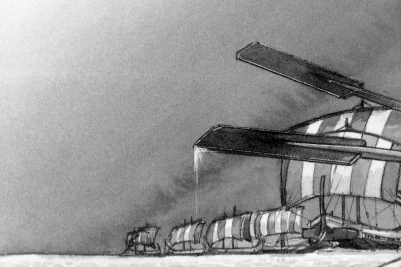

On the way to Troy, the Greeks landed at the island of Tenedos. There, the archer Philoctetes was bitten on the foot by a snake. His wound was so bad that the Greeks left him there against his will.

For Helen, the woman whose face has launched 1,000 ships!

Ask the storyteller

What made Achilles so special?

Everyone knew that Achilles was the strongest hero of all. When he was a baby, his mother had dipped him in the waters of the River Styx. The water was to make it so no harm could ever come to her son. However, his heel had not touched the water. This would later prove to be his weak spot.

The Siege of Troy

When the army came ashore, the people of Troy looked down on the Greeks from the strong walls the gods had helped build. Agamemnon and his men made camp outside the city. A siege began, which would last for 10 long years.

In the 10th year, Agamemnon captured a girl called Chryseis and would not release her. Unfortunately, her father was one of Apollo's priests. Agamemnon's actions angered the god, and Apollo sent a deadly plague upon the Greek army.

The Greeks feared for their lives. Achilles called a crisis meeting at which it was decreed that Agamemnon should return Chryseis. Agamemnon did this, but to make up for his loss, he stole Achilles's favorite slave girl, Briseis. This caused a great argument between the two men. In anger, Achilles refused to have anything else to do with the fight against the Trojans. This was a terrible blow for Agamemnon. He remembered the prophecy that Troy could not be conquered without Achilles.

The first Greek on Troy's shore

There was a prophecy that said the first Greek to set foot on Trojan soil would be the first to die in battle. Knowing this, the wily Odysseus, who was first to leave the ships, threw his shield to the ground and stood on it. Though Protesilaus followed Odysseus out, he was the first to tread on land. The prophecy was fulfilled, and Protesilaus was the first Greek soldier to be killed.

Ask the storyteller

Did the Greeks give peace a chance?

Even after the war started, the Greeks sent ambassadors who asked for Helen and the stolen treasure to be returned. Yet the Trojans would not listen. Instead, they insulted the Greeks. From behind the safety of the city walls, they threw garbage down on them.

Let the Battle Begin!

Even though the plague had claimed the lives of many Greeks, and Achilles was not fighting alongside him, Agamemnon chose to fight on. It was a bad choice to make. Achilles was still sulking because Agamemnon had stolen Briseis, Achilles's slave girl. Agamemnon didn't know it, but the vengeful Achilles had called on the gods to punish him. The gods answered Achilles's call, and for a time they let the Trojans defeat Agamemnon's army in one struggle after another. It looked as if the Trojans would win the war and send the Greeks back empty-handed. Many things happened in the 10th year of the Trojan War ....

A lucky escape!

A truce was called so that Paris and Menelaus could fight a duel. The winner would take Helen, and the war would end. However, when Menelaus was about to kill Paris, the goddess Aphrodite, who was on Paris's side, made him vanish.

Athena interferes

The goddess Athena did not want the war to stop. She disguised herself as a Trojan and persuaded an archer to fire an arrow from the walls of Troy. His arrow struck Menelaus and wounded him. Firing an arrow broke the truce, and so the war started up again.

Assassination!

The Greek heroes Odysseus and Diomedes killed Rhesus, king of the Thracians, who was fighting on the side of the Trojans. They stole his prized white horses, which shone as bright as sunbeams, were as fast as the wind, and could become invisible.

Thersites the coward

Thersites, the ugliest of the Greeks, demanded that Agamemnon abandon the war so that the men could return home safely to Greece. No one took any notice of Thersites. Odysseus beat him with his staff until Thersites apologized for speaking out.

An even fight

Ajax, a mighty Greek, fought a duel with Hector, the bravest of the Trojans. The fight lasted all day, with neither man winning. When night fell, they exchanged gifts and parted as equals.

Ask the storyteller

Where was Achilles while all this was happening?

Because of his argument with Agamemnon, Achilles, the bravest of all the Greeks, angrily refused to take part in the fight. Instead, he stayed inside his tent with his friend Patroclus.

The fleet in flames

With help from the gods, Hector broke through the Greeks' defenses on the beach and set their ships on fire. For as long as Achilles stayed out of the fighting, the gods helped the Trojans beat the Greeks.

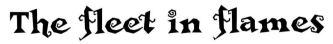

17

Achilles Kills Hector

With the war going against them, the Greeks feared the gods had deserted them—which they had! Their only hope of victory rested with Achilles. Agamemnon called on the hero to return to the war, promising to give Briseis back. He offered him treasure. He promised him 20 of the most beautiful women of Troy. He even offered the hand of one of his own daughters in marriage. Achilles, still sulking, refused all of Agamemnon's gifts.

When Hector the Trojan burned the Greeks' ships, Achilles's friend Patroclus begged to return to the fight. Achilles lent his own armor to Patroclus. Achilles hoped to fool the Trojans into thinking it was actually he who was fighting. Hector was far stronger than Patroclus, though, and soon killed him. Overcome with grief at the death of his friend, Achilles told Agamemnon their quarrel was over and that he would return to the war.

Wearing a new suit of armor, Achilles pursued Hector around the walls of Troy. Finally they fought, and Achilles killed his enemy with a spear through his throat. He tied Hector's lifeless body to his chariot and dragged it around Troy, so the Trojans would see that their greatest warrior was dead.

Achilles's armor

After Hector had killed Patroclus, he stripped Achilles's armor from his dead body and wore it as his own. Achilles grieved for Patroclus, and he arranged a grand funeral for him, at which 12 Trojans were sacrificed to the gods. When Achilles killed Hector, he took his armor back.

Ask the storyteller

What happened to Hector's body?

Achilles dragged Hector's body behind his chariot for many days. Dogs and birds picked at it. Only when Priam, the king of Troy, paid a ransom was the body returned to his people. Hector was given a hero's funeral, and there was a truce that lasted 12 days.

The Greeks will be victorious!

The Death of Achilles

Now that Achilles was back fighting, the war at last turned in favor of the Greeks. They began to defeat their Trojan enemy. Penthesilea, queen of the Amazons, came to fight with the Trojans. She was no match for Achilles, though, and he cut her down.

Achilles's days were numbered, too. Although everyone believed he couldn't be harmed, he did have a weak spot. When Achilles and Paris met in combat, Apollo guided the Trojan's arrow toward the one part of Achilles's body left unprotected by the waters of the River Styx. The arrow struck Achilles in the heel and his life drained away. The hero of the Greeks was dead. Mighty Ajax carried Achilles's body to the Greeks' camp, where Achilles was mourned for 17 days. His body was then burned on a funeral pyre and his ashes mixed with those of his friend Patroclus.

Paris is killed

Philoctetes, abandoned on the island of Tenedos, was keeper of the bow and arrows of Hercules. He entered the war when Odysseus stole the weapons. Philoctetes followed Odysseus, who led him to Troy. With a poisoned arrow shot from the bow of Hercules, Philoctetes killed Paris.

My...life... is...over...

Ask the storyteller

What happened to Ajax?

A contest was held to see who should be given Achilles's armor. Ajax expected to win, but he lost out to Odysseus. In a moment of despair and madness, he killed the sheep that the Greeks kept for food. Afraid of being mocked, Ajax put his sword in the ground, fell on it, and killed himself.

The Wooden Horse of Troy

As it turned out, the Greeks had captured a Trojan prophet who could see into the future. He said three things must happen if the Greeks were to capture Troy: They must bring Philoctetes to fight with them. The son of Achilles must fight in the war, and a sacred statue must be stolen from the Trojans. So much for the Trojan prophet's prediction. Even after the three conditions were met, the siege continued.

It was the goddess Athena who told the Greeks what to do. On her instructions, they built a huge wooden horse inside which 12 Greek soldiers hid. These words were written on the horse: "For their return home, the Greeks dedicate this as thanks to Athena." The horse was dragged to Troy and left outside its gates. Then, the rest of the Greek army boarded its ships and sailed away, pretending to abandon the war. One man called Sinon stayed behind as a decoy.

The next morning, the Trojans could not believe their luck—the Greeks had gone! Sinon, who had let them capture him, told them that the horse was a gift to Athena. He said that the horse was too big for the Trojans to take inside their city. This made the Trojans more eager to bring it within the walls of Troy and prove the Greek wrong.

Twelve brave men

No one knows how many men were hidden inside the wooden horse. The story is so old that the number is long forgotten. Some say there were 23 or 30, others say 50, 100, or even 3,000. This story goes by 12.

Ask the storyteller

Was everyone fooled by the Greeks' trickery?

Although some Trojans were suspicious about the Greeks' "gift," only one man spoke out. He was a priest called Laocoon. However, the goddess Athena sent two giant sea serpents, which killed Laocoon and his two sons. The people thought that this was punishment for refusing the gift.

Come on, Sinon, tell us the truth.

The horse will fit if you say so...

The Fall of Troy

The only way the horse could be brought into Troy was by taking down part of the city wall. With this done, the horse was dragged through the gap. The Trojans finally celebrated because they thought victory was theirs.

Inside the wooden horse, the Greek soldiers stayed still and quiet. They waited until nightfall when the Trojans were asleep. Then they crept from their hiding place. From high up on the walls of Troy, Helen—the woman over whom the war had been fought —lit a torch. Its flame was seen from far away by the Greek army. This was their signal that the city was open to attack, and the fleet sailed back to the walled city.

The Greeks destroyed the city, ransacked its temples, and looted its treasures. Priam, the king of Troy, was killed. Hecabe, his wife, and Cassandra, his daughter, were taken prisoner. The baby son of Hector, the Trojans' fallen warrior, was thrown from the city walls, and his wife became a captive of the victorious Greeks.

Why Helen helped the Greeks

Helen had lived in Troy for many years. She had become the wife of Paris, the Trojan who had tricked her into leaving Sparta. In all this time, she had wished to return to Greece. Odysseus told her that if she betrayed the Trojans, her wish would come true.

24

Ask the storyteller

What happened to Helen?

Let us not forget that the Trojan War started because the Trojans had taken Helen, the most beautiful woman in the world, away from Menelaus, her husband. But, this story has a happy ending. With the fall of Troy, Helen was reunited with Menelaus.

25

The Return of the Heroes

After 10 years of war, the Greek heroes hoped to be home in a few days, but this was not to be. The gods were angry with the Greeks. They had not wanted Troy—a city they had helped build—to be destroyed. They regarded the destruction of its temples as an act of sacrilege.

So, in punishment, the gods sent a great storm to batter the returning Greek fleet. Many ships were sunk, leaving only a few to reach safety. One was Agamemnon's ship, which was protected by the goddess Hera. Though he returned to his palace, a surprise awaited him. While he had been away, his wife, Clytemnestra, had fallen in love with another man. She no longer wanted Agamemnon, so she murdered him while he was bathing.

Athena's anger

The goddess Athena had supported the Greeks all through the war, but she was angry when they turned Troy to rubble. She decided to punish them with storms.

Ask the storyteller

Did Helen and Menelaus live happily ever after?

After the storm, it took seven long years for Menelaus and Helen to travel home. When they finally returned to Sparta, they had been away from the city for a total of 17 years. They spent the rest of their lives there. When Menelaus was old, Zeus took him to the lovely and peaceful Elysian fields, and Apollo made Helen into a goddess.

The End of the Story?

And so we reach the end of our storyteller's tale. However, the end of one story is often the beginning of the next. From the ruins of Troy came forth a Trojan hero —a leader who had fought the Greeks. His name was Aeneas. He fled the city, carrying his lame father, Anchises, on his shoulders, and his young son, Ascanius, in his arms. He also took with him special objects that were sacred to the gods of Troy.

He traveled far looking for a place to found a new kingdom. He moved to Thrace, then to Delos and then to Crete, but he was not destined to settle in any of these places. Nor was he to find peace in Sicily, the island where his father died. Only when he reached Italy did his fortune change. He came to the River Tiber and entered the region ruled by King Latinus. Aeneas married the king's daughter, Lavinia, and founded a city that he named Lavinium in her honor. When Aeneas's son, Ascanius, was a man, he too founded a city in Italy. Many years later, Romulus, a descendant of Aeneas, founded yet another city called Rome. All these years later, Rome stands as the capital of Italy.

Aeneas, father of the Romans

It was predicted that one day Aeneas would eat the plate his food came on. This would happen at his new home. On the banks of the River Tiber in Italy, Aeneas ate the thin loaf of bread he was using as a plate. It was there that he founded the city of Lavinium.

Ask the storyteller

What happened to Troy?

With its royal family dead, its population killed or sold into slavery, the city of Troy was in ruins, never to be lived in again. All that is left is its distant memory, which is kept alive through stories such as this one.

Glossary

Amazons A race of warrior women who lived in Asia.

Ambassador An official sent to talk to the leaders of a foreign country.

Duel An arranged fight between two people.

Elysian fields The Greek version of heaven, where good people spent their afterlife.

Immortal A being who cannot die, such as a god.

Lame Unable to walk.

Mortal A being who will die one day or who can be killed.

Omen A sign that points to future events.

Oracle A person who can tell what will happen in the future.

Prophecy A tale of what will happen in the future.

Prophet Someone who tells a prophecy.

Pyre A platform on which corpses are burned.

Ransom A payment for somebody's safe return.

River Styx A river in the Underworld, which is where ancient Greeks believed people went when they died.

Sacrilege A crime against the gods.

Suitor A man who is seeking a woman's hand in marriage.

Truce An agreement to stop fighting.

Who's Who

Achilles (uh-KILL-eez) The strongest Greek soldier at Troy.

Aeacus (EE-a-kus) A mortal who helped the gods build the walls of Troy.

Aeneas (en-EE-as) A Trojan who became father of the Romans.

Agamemnon (ag-ah-MEM-non) Leader of the Greek army and Menelaus's brother.

Ajax (AY-jax) A Greek hero with great strength.

Anchises (an-KEY-seez) Father of Aeneas.

Aphrodite (aff-ro-DY-tee) Goddess of love.

Apollo (uh-POL-oh) God of medicine and music.

Artemis (ARE-tuh-miss) Goddess of hunting.

Ascanius (as-KAN-ee-us) Son of Aeneas.

Athena (uh-THEE-na) Goddess of war.

Briseis (bry-SEE-is) A slave girl who belonged to Achilles.

Calchas (KAL-kass) A fortune-teller.

Cassandra (kass-AN-dra) Daughter of Priam.

Chryseis (cry-SEE-is) A slave girl who belonged to Agamemnon.

Clytemnestra (kly-tum-NESS-tra) Wife of Agamemnon.

Diomedes (dy-o-MEE-deez) A leader of the Greeks.

Eris (AIR-iss) Goddess of strife.

Hecabe (HEK-ah-bee) Wife of Priam and queen of Troy.

Hector (HEK-tore) The strongest Trojan soldier.

Helen (HEL-un) Wife of Menelaus.

Hera (HEE-ra) Wife of Zeus and queen of the gods.

Hercules (HER-cue-leez) A Greek hero with great strength.

Hesione (hess-EYE-on-ee) Daughter of Laomedon.

Iphigeneia (iff-uh-gen-EE-ah) Daughter of Agamemnon.

Laocoon (lay-CO-on) A priest in Troy.

Laomedon (lay-OH-me-don) Father of Priam and Hesione.

Lavinia (la-VIN-ee-ah) Wife of Aeneas.

Menelaus (me-ne-LAY-us) Helen's husband.

Odysseus (oh-DISS-ee-us) A Greek hero.

Paris (PA-riss) Son of Priam; Helen's kidnapper.

Patroclus (pa-TRO-klus) Best friend of Achilles.

Penthesilea (pen-thess-ILL-ee-ah) Queen of the Amazons.

Philoctetes (fi-lok-TEE-teez) Keeper of the bow and arrows of Hercules.

Podarces (po-DAR-seez) Original name of Priam.

Poseidon (poss-EYE-don) God of the sea.

Priam (PRY-am) King of Troy and Paris's father.

Protesilaus (proh-tess-ill-AY-us) The first Greek to die in the Trojan War.

Rhesus (REE-suss) A Thracian king.

Sinon (SY-non) A Greek spy.

Thersites (thur-SY-teez) An ugly Greek soldier.

Tyndareus (tin-DAR-yoos) Father of Helen.

Zeus (ZOOS) King of the gods.

Index

A

Achilles, 12–13, 14, 16–17, 18–19, 20–21, 22, 31
Aeacus, 6, 31
Aeneas, 28, 31
Agamemnon, 12, 14, 16–17, 18, 26, 31
Ajax, 17, 20–21, 31
Amazons, 20, 30, 31
Anchises, 28, 31
Aphrodite, 8, 10–11, 16, 31
Apollo, 6, 14, 20, 27, 31
armor, of Achilles, 18, 21
Ascanius, 28, 31
Athena, 8, 16, 22–23, 26, 31
Aulis, 4, 12

B

Briseis, 14, 16, 18, 31

C

Calchas, 12, 14, 31
Cassandra, 24, 31
Chryseis, 14, 31
Clytemnestra, 26, 31

D

Diomedes, 17, 31

E

Elysian fields, 27, 30
Eris, 8, 31

G

golden apple, 8

H

Hecabe, 8, 24, 31
Hector, 17, 18–19, 24, 31
heel, of Achilles, 13, 20
Helen, 8–9, 10–11, 12, 15, 16, 24, 25, 27, 31
Hera, 8, 26, 31
Hercules, 6–7, 20, 31
Hesione, 6–7, 31
horses, of Laomedon, 6–7
horses, of Rhesus, 17

I

Iphigeneia, 12, 31
Italy, 28

L

Laocoon, 23, 31
Laomedon, 6, 7, 31
Lavinia, 28, 31
Lavinium, 28

M

marriage, of Helen, 10
Menelaus, 10–11, 12, 16, 25, 27, 31
Mycenae, 4, 10, 12

O

Odysseus, 14, 17, 20–21, 24, 31
omen, 8, 12, 30
oracle, 6, 30

P

Paris, 8–9, 10–11, 16, 20, 24, 31
Patroclus, 17, 18, 20, 31
Penthesilea, 20, 31
Philoctetes, 12, 20, 22, 31
plague, 6, 14, 16
Podarces, 7, 31
Poseidon, 6, 31
Priam, 7, 8, 19, 24, 31
prophecy, 12, 14, 30
prophet, 12, 22, 30
Protesilaus, 14, 31

R

rhapsode, 5
Rhesus, 17, 31
Rome, 28
Romulus, 28

S

serpent, 6, 23
Sinon, 22, 31
snakes, 6, 12
Sparta, 4, 10, 24, 27
Styx, River, 13, 20, 30

T

Tenedos, 12, 20
Thersites, 17, 31
Tiber, River, 28
truce, 16, 19, 30
Tyndareus, 10, 31

W

wooden horse, 22, 24

Z

Zeus, 6, 8, 27, 31